NOT *Just* ANOTHER *Marriage Book*

EXPLODE YOUR RELATIONSHIP

DOUG AND SISSY PITCHER

STELLAR
COMMUNICATIONS
HOUSTON

NOT JUST ANOTHER MARRIAGE BOOK:
EXPLODE YOUR RELATIONSHIP

Unless otherwise noted, all Scripture references and quotations are taken from
the New King James Version (NKJV), Copyright © 1982 by Thomas Nelson.

Printed in the United States of America
First Printing, April 2017

Library of Congress Control Number: 2017941677

ISBN 978-0-9989422-0-9 (Paperback)
ISBN 978-0-9989422-1-6 (E-book)

Stellar Communications Houston
www.stellarwriter.com
281-804-7089

Preparation for publication by Ella Hearrean Ritchie
Author portrait by Amanda Freeman Photography
Cover design by Alejandro Bisogno & Elena Reznikova
Interior design by Elena Reznikova

Cover Stock Images:
Vintage Tone Cross on a Hill: © aradaphotography / 123RF Stock Photo
Hands in the Shape of a Heart: © rufphotography / 123RF Stock Photo

More Praise for *Not Just Another Marriage Book*

"A must have for individuals preparing their hearts for marriage! It is insightful, practical, and a great navigating tool for couples who want to enjoy the full measure of a healthy relationship and bypass the unnecessary pitfalls of hurt and incompatibility. This is a great resource for pastors and counselors!"

—Lenda Crawford
Women's Ministry, The Freedom Center Church,
Missouri City, Texas

"Doug and Sissy Pitcher of Pitcher Ministries have identified a much neglected problem area in our society regarding marital relationships. Their inspired teachings and guidance in *Not Just Another Marriage Book* is priceless, helping to avoid pitfalls that lead to unhealthy relationships. This is for you if you want to know how to identify the right mate and avoid all-too-common mistakes during the pre-marital experience. This easy-to-read book also gives important principles, sometimes humorous analogies, and examples to apply if you're intentional about having a healthy marriage. I'm excited about the positive impact this book will have on the many couples who will learn God's design for marriage."

—Barbara Yvonne Long
Educator (Retired) and Bible Studies Teacher,
Missouri City, Texas

"If you want to truly unlock the God-given power hidden in your current or future marriage, this book is a must-read. Marriage was created by God to provide the support and power needed for families to reach their full God-given potential in every area of their lives, and this book is packed with foundational keys required to achieve that goal. Doug and Sissy share their hearts with genuine love and transparency to help others learn from the mistakes they experienced and keep them from experiencing similar heartache. That is a rare and valuable gift that can have a life-changing impact for those willing to make the investment in themselves. Their approach is very practical, even humorous at times, and can be applied to any romantic relationship in which one or both parties want to build a God-centered marriage and experience all of its benefits. I encourage you to take the time to read and study this book and invite God into your relationship."

—Antoinette Campbell
Kingdom Families Facilitator,
Richmond, Texas

"I've known Doug and Sissy Pitcher as intensely committed teachers to the "how" of having a long-lasting marriage relationship. Best of all, these teachings come personally from their own experiences in dealing with marriages, including their own. They've proven their commitment to building successful marriages, as we've observed their daily walk with the Lord in our church."

—Clarence A. Lee, Jr.
Pastor Emeritus, The Freedom Center Church,
Missouri City, Texas

"The Pitchers remind me of Proverbs 27:17: "As iron sharpens iron. . . ." Doug and Sissy are truly anointed in their ministry. They bring passion, fun, laughter, and truth to their teaching and Biblically address topics in a way that is a blessing in disguise. Their wisdom and personal testimonies sharpen the marriages they touch, including ours. We are forever grateful for how they have touched our lives."

—James and Jennifer Bowling
Independent Business Advisors, Spring, Texas

Dedication

We dedicate this work to God, our Heavenly Father; our Lord and Savior, Jesus Christ; and to our family and friends who have supported us through our journey. We thank God for the call He has placed on us as we reach individuals and couples through Pitcher Ministries, Inc., "Pouring God's Design into Relationships."

This message of hope and encouragement is dedicated to our readers as they desire to explode their relationships for eternity.

Contents

Foreword   ix

Preface   xi

Acknowledgements   xv

Introduction   xix

Chapter 1: EDUCATE   1

Chapter 2: X-RAY   13

Chapter 3: PURSUE   27

Chapter 4: LOVE   33

Chapter 5: OPERATE   45

Chapter 6: DESIGN   55

Chapter 7: EXPECT   63

Afterword   69

Bibliography   73

Letter to the Reader   75

About the Authors   77

Foreword

I can honestly say that I know the Pitchers' hearts in writing this book. Their hearts are in union with mine in that we would not see another marriage run off the road and meet an unnecessary demise. God has in fact designed marriage and given us the tools to be successful. So whatever state your relationship or marriage might resemble right now, God has laid out the road map to successfully navigate a lasting and fulfilling relationship. It's possible, attainable, and should be expected that no matter the trials or difficulties along the road, two people can succeed in love by following God's plan.

In Doug and Sissy Pitcher's book, *Not Just Another Marriage Book: Explode Your Relationship,* you will find a very practical and thoughtful guide designed to assist couples in successfully overcoming the challenges and pitfalls most couples encounter.

No matter where your relationship is, you will feel empowered, enlightened, and equipped as you understand God's design to EXPLODE your love and partnership.

Read the book. Do the work, and you will not be disappointed. The best way to get to your destination successfully and efficiently is through pre-trip planning. This book is for everyone who is married, engaged to be married, or looking to be married. Pre-plan that journey! This book will be a great guide to make your marriage beautiful, exciting, and most of all successful. All of these adjectives describe a marriage that brings God glory because that is exactly how He designed marriage to be.

—Greg Crawford
Senior Pastor, The Freedom Center Church
Missouri City, Texas

Preface

The title of this book, *Not Just Another Marriage Book: Explode Your Relationship,* was dropped into our hearts as we were discussing writing the book. Doug casually stated, "We do not want this to be just another marriage book." The Lord then impressed upon us that this desire was our title. Our marriages become "not just another marriage" when we intentionally explode our relationships. Having both been divorced and having gone through the hurt and healing process of all that comes with divorce, we have a strong passion to educate individuals before they marry and during those early years of marriage. It is through our past pains and failures that God called us to form Pitcher Ministries Inc. This call is coupled with the desire to strengthen couples on the front-end of marriage striving to help eliminate the need for damage control years down the road.

Our hearts cringe as we see many couples plow straight into a marriage with their "eyes tightly closed." We want to help couples go into marriage with their "eyes wide open." As we have questioned numerous married couples today, a common thread is lurking behind many of their challenges. They simply say, "We had no clue, no education, and we only wish we would have known then what we know now." We are on a mission to help individuals to the best of their abilities form beautiful and fulfilling marriage relationships. Without a doubt, there are many people with failed marriages who would tell you after the fact that they knew things were not completely right, but they thought it would get better after marriage. Sad to say, the majority did not get better. The relationships spiraled into deeper problems, many times ending in divorce.

As in all facets of life, if we want to succeed at something, we need to investigate it and grow in our knowledge of that particular area. Marriage is no different! Many times we have simply focused on the wedding day and overlooked the need to invest in the growth of our relationships. Consequently, we are not seeking the necessary tools and equipment we need to have a successful and fulfilling marriage. It is definitely not our goal to simply have couples "stay married." Quite the contrary, we want couples to marry and thrive in their marriages. We want couples to excel and receive all that God originally intended for them! Our hearts' desire is for couples to enjoy their marriages till "death do us part." And yes, that is possible even today!

Marriage was created to be a blessing to ALL who enter in: this is attainable IF you are pursuing marriage as intended by the Creator. This book will help guide you down the pathway that a marriage relationship was originally created to travel. As you read through the pages, you will discover how exploding your relationship can have a very positive effect.

Are you aggressive or passive in the direction of your marriage? Do you want a healthier and more vibrant marriage? Buy the book, apply the Word of God, and allow God to *EXPLODE* your relationship to the next level and soar with the eagles. When applying the Biblical concepts in this book to *your* marriage, you will enjoy a relationship in which both parties *intentionally* encourage each other to attain their full potential in Christ! As you both are transforming into the image of Christ, you will continue to become *ONE*. No longer should marriages settle for status quo, *just another marriage.* Instead, we need to receive what God intended for each of us.

Acknowledgements

We first want to thank God, our Heavenly Father, for lovingly bringing us together in a covenant marriage. Through this beautiful union, He has walked with us, and we are now seeing His purpose and plan for us as a couple be fulfilled. We also thank Jesus Christ, our Lord and Savior, who is our Elder Brother and the One we want to imitate in our daily walks.

Along our journey, God blessed us with a rock-solid church family at The Freedom Center Church in Missouri City, Texas. As we have walked through life's challenges, this loving church family has supported us through prayer, encouragement, financial contributions, listening ears, and simply love. Thank you to our previous pastors, Curry and Beverly Juneau, who were always standing on truth and living it out in front of us. Our current pastors, Greg and Lenda Crawford, have come right in behind them and not missed a step. The transparency of their own lives and their love for God and His creation is always guiding us into deeper walks with Him. We have been privileged to sit under a ministry that preaches truth no matter how society changes. We are grateful and thankful for the leadership that The Freedom Center Church has provided us.

There are times in life when God gives us a very special friend and mentor who challenges us to soar with the eagles and not quit. Barbara Long is truly that friend (family) for us. Despite our obstacles, Barbara has encouraged us as we endeavored to write this book, praying countless hours on our behalf and depriving herself of her time to pour into us. She has propelled us to keep on no matter what. Our bond with Barbara is one that only God can bring into people's lives. We are forever blessed and grateful for this special friendship and all that she has endured and walked through with us.

To Jennifer Bowling and Antoinette Campbell, we thank you from the bottom of our hearts for taking your valuable time to help us accomplish our undertaking of this work. You are beautiful women of God, and your lives are a reflection of Him. We are grateful for your proofing and encouraging comments. We are blessed to be walking our journey with friends like you.

Thank you to Alejandro (Ally) Bisogno for the beautifully created cover for our book. Ally is a young woman of God with a great gifting of creativity. She worked numerous hours hammering out a stunning cover, and we are grateful for our paths crossing. We look forward to Ally stepping out into her God-given gift for the Kingdom. We know God has a bright future planned for this vibrant young woman of God.

We have saved our family for last. We have been blessed with parents who have loved us, cared for us, and nurtured us throughout our lives. Without this love and care, we would not be where we are today. We dearly love and thank our parents, Austin and Donna Pitcher, Jay (Coach) and Georgia Ann Spears and the late Johnnie Ruffeno, Sr. We are blessed with six wonderful children: Rebecca Gush, Rachel Mangum, Klaire Brown, Tiffany Bittner, David Pitcher, and Melinda Pitcher. We are also the proud grandparents to Madeline, Addison and Emerson Bittner, Maxwell Brown, and Seamus Gush. Each of our children and grandchildren holds a special place in our hearts. Our love for each of them extends far and wide. Our children and grandchildren continue to motivate us to stay in the Word. It is our desire to leave behind a legacy of faith that continues on after we are called home. We thank God for each of you, and we love you dearly.

Introduction

Living in this unbelievably fast-paced, high-achieving world today definitely comes with its stresses. As we have talked with many individuals, married and single, a common thread they share is feeling stressed and overwhelmed. Unfortunately, much of this turmoil finds its way into our relationships, especially our marriages. As we press forward, striving to reach our goals, we struggle with our ability to balance all that our hearts desire. Many times our most important relationships suffer from this lack of time.

Why would we allow our most important relationships to suffer? Could it be because we feel that if anyone will understand our time issues, surely it is our spouses, fiancés, or significant others? After all, they "love" us and need to "cut us some slack." Although love is present and grace is extended, many times our lack of time or energy to nurture our relationships is dangerous for the quality of life enjoyed as a couple. Before we know it, our very special relationships become emotional roller coasters and, quite frankly, high maintenance and stressful.

Relationships come in all shapes and sizes. Most

married couples would say their marriage is the most important relationship to them. Believers might say their marriage relationship is the second most important relationship to them, with Jesus Christ being the first. If this is the case, how then is it that we would neglect our highly valued relationships? We can safely say this neglect is rarely intentional. As a matter of fact, many do not even realize the neglect exists until their relationships are in a severe downward spiral.

If you were asked to be completely honest about your marriage relationship, how would you classify it?

1. Challenging to say the least. (A "stick shift" car with lots of jerks when changing gears.)
2. Not what you thought it would be. (A "lemon" car that was great during the test drive, but over time unexpected issues have appeared.)
3. Exceeds your expectations. (A "luxury" car that is smooth and reliable.)

Now we did say be COMPLETELY honest. Unfortunately, many relationships are not in the "luxury" car category. How do we draw this conclusion? Statistics in our world today prove many marriages are far from a smooth ride. What would you say if we told you it is time to **EXPLODE** your relationship?

Before you go negative on us and stop reading this book, hear us out. Would you like to **EXPLODE** your current relationship into something along the "smooth and reliable" line? Many of us married without a clue as to what the original design of marriage truly is about. It is our desire to help educate and enlighten individuals on the intention of the original design of marriage.

Commit to yourself (if single) or to each other to read this short book with an open heart and open mind. We want to challenge you to **EXPLODE** your relationship into what God intended for you. We are going to **E**ducate, **X**-ray, **P**ursue, **L**ove, **O**perate, **D**esign and **E**xpect our marriages and relationships to excel with God's design. Allow the Creator Himself to guide you into His perfect design for your relationship.

Do any of the reasons below sound like anything you have heard or felt before marrying?

1. He or she completes me.
2. He or she is my best friend.
3. We share common interests.
4. We share the same values.
5. He or she will always be with me physically, emotionally, and spiritually.
6. We "really love" each other, so we won't end up like other couples.
7. This is my soul mate.
8. I don't ever want to live without him or her.
9. He or she truly understands (gets) me.
10. Our love is all we need.

Obviously, this is not a complete list of reasons that people give for marriage, but you should get the point. Although all of these reasons may be true in your relationship TODAY, did you consider the fact that we all change along life's way? Yes, even you will change as the years go by. Not one of us will remain the exact same throughout life. We are not simply talking about the physical changes that we all will face, but also our thought processes. Maybe your relationship has all ten of these attributes or a combination of several. However, these factors in and of themselves cannot and will not guarantee a reliable, fulfilling relationship for the rest of your life. There **MUST** and **IS** a greater, stronger foundation to sustain our marriage relationships!

Let's back up a minute. . . . "What is a relationship?" *Merriam-Webster's Collegiate Dictionary* defines the word relationship as: "(1) The way in which two or more people, groups, countries, etc. talk to, behave toward, and deal with each other; (2) A romantic or sexual friendship between two people, and (3) The way in which two or more people or things are connected." As you read these definitions, someone most likely comes to your mind.

Next question: "How did the marriage relationship start?" In the first book of the Bible, Genesis 2:24 says, "Therefore a man shall leave his father and mother and be joined to his wife, and they shall become one flesh." THIS is where the institution of marriage was created, and we should add . . . by the Creator! God is the creator of marriage, not man. Are we to believe that God created marriage so it could be the failure it is in so many of our lives today? No way! We know God is a giver of only good gifts (James 1:17), so we know marriage was NEVER intended by God to be a struggle that brings more stress into our lives. Quite the contrary, marriage is a gift and a blessing.

Why then does it appear that marriage, as most know it today, is not highly regarded or cherished? Why is it that in many conversations today marriage is mocked, laughed at, and viewed as a curse—or better yet a "death sentence"? Why are so many (even in the church) opting to live together, not wanting to commit to a marriage? Why is there such a negative stigma with marriage today? We would submit that a large majority of marriages today, even in the church, are not *intentionally* following God's pathway for their marriages. Therefore, marriage is not being pursued in the way it was created to be pursued. We do not have to look very hard to see the damaging results this has caused in our society.

God's ways are higher than our ways. The world's ways do not, nor have they ever, lined up with God's ways. Therefore, when entering or maintaining a marriage relationship following God's design, it is not going to be with the same approach as the couple who disregards God completely or the couple who has "a form of godliness but denies the power thereof" (2 Timothy 3:5). This Scripture refers to those going to church but not really seeking God's plan for them, those who love God but just are not desiring to go deeper into His plan for them.

John 3:16 is a very popular verse in the Bible stating, "For God so loved the world, that He gave his only begotten son, that whosoever believeth in him should not perish, but have everlasting life." As Believers, this unbelievable act of love still is astonishing and incomprehensible. God, as well as Jesus, truly is an example of how individuals should love and be committed in a relationship. The very fact that God so desired a relationship with us that He would have His only son die for us is beyond comprehension. This type of love will keep a relationship through the highs and lows of life. This is the type of love that we all should be striving to attain.

When we want a driver's license, we learn all the rules and consequences of driving the roads so we can pass the driver's license test. If we desire to become a nurse, fireman, police officer, teacher, attorney, or CPA, we find the best educational training possible to achieve our goals or career paths. And we need to add that we place great value on this training and therefore are willing to pay high dollar for this teaching! It is important to note as well that all of the above careers have a test that must be passed. Does it not make sense that when we decide to get married, we should also pursue the best educational material to be successful in our marriages? How fantastic it is that we have the ability to educate ourselves on marriage without even paying tuition!

Do you think more people would educate themselves on marriage if there were a test before you could marry? What if we could not get married if we did not pass the test? Would we be willing then to put in the time and effort to learn about our relationships?

It is our belief that many young singles and couples know early on if they intend to become married or remain single. The complexity of two becoming one flesh is definitely something we need help to accomplish. Remember, there is only one YOU! This means that in a marriage we have two different individuals becoming one. This was and is God's design, not man's design! Therefore, the only real expert on success in marriage is the Creator of marriage, God. God obviously has a great plan for a man and a woman in marriage. Unfortunately, sin and the influence of society have totally distorted His plan. Although this distortion of marriage exists today, it does not change the fact that God is a giver of good gifts and marriage is indeed one of those good gifts.

Most likely by now you have figured out that the only way to achieve a truly smooth and reliable marriage relationship is by following the Creator's design. Why would one want to get advice from any other source than the Creator of marriage Himself? If you are driving a brand new Lexus and encounter a problem with it, will you run your car to the Chevrolet dealer and ask them to look at it? Most likely not. Why? Simply because the Lexus dealer is the designer and manufacturer of your vehicle, and they are the experts on your car. You certainly would not read the *Chevrolet Owner's Manual* when you purchase a Lexus, would you?

In the following few chapters, we want to encourage you to join with us as we **EXPLODE** our current relationships. We are not suggesting you have a bad relationship; however, we are suggesting that **all** relationships have room for growth. Regardless if you are single and know you want to marry one day, dating seriously, engaged, newlyweds, or married for a long time, we know there is something in this book that will benefit your relationship.

Please pray this prayer with us: *Father, we come to You in the name of Jesus, asking You to open our hearts, spirits, and minds to all that You have for us as individuals and couples. Help us rid our relationships of those things that block us from enjoying Your full benefits of our marriage covenants. It is our hearts' desire to become one and pursue our relationships as You originally created them to be. We thank You for Your faithfulness and look forward to the positive results You will provide us. In Jesus' name, Amen.*

CHAPTER ONE

EDUCATE

M ost of us are familiar with the word **EDUCATE,** or education, especially since we are required by law to educate our children for twelve years. Failure to do this can result in criminal charges. According to *Merriam-Webster's Collegiate Dictionary*, one definition of educate is "to develop mentally, morally, or aesthetically especially by instruction."

Let's do a little introspection. . . . "Can you say that you spent any or much time educating yourself on marriage BEFORE marrying?" We are not talking about a required pre-marital counseling period with your pastor or counselor at the church. We are talking about your intentional education on an upcoming marriage relationship. Preparing yourself for a mate. If so, where did this education come from? Was it from the Creator's design plan? Hosea 4:6 states, "My people are destroyed from a lack of knowledge." This might be one of the largest—if not **the** largest reason— we see so many destroyed marriages today. How can any of us expect to enjoy the blessing that marriage is intended to be when we have not educated ourselves regarding marriage? Again, if we want to be lawyers and never attend law school, we will not be lawyers because the law itself requires us to go to school and pass the bar.

Where can we find accurate information that truly helps educate us on marriage relationships? Right, you guessed it: the Bible. This is where we can discover the intended blessings and responsibilities of marriage. We find that God decided it was not good for man to live alone and created woman. We see that this woman was created to be a helper for the man; we might say "teamwork" (Genesis 2:18). In the beginning of their relationship, prior to their sin, there was such purity that they were naked, not just physically, but openly and honestly as well (Genesis 2:25). This is how God created them. It was God's plan for a man to focus on his new marriage and bring happiness to his bride (Deuteronomy 24:5). Men were to enjoy their wives (Ecclesiastes 9:9). A husband should love his wife as Christ loved the church, and a wife should respect her husband (Ephesians 5:33). We cannot forget the other blessing in marriage, the big one that is always talked about: **sex**

(1 Corinthians 7:1-3). Lastly, but certainly not lacking importance, marriage was created to be honored (Hebrews 13:4-7). This is not a complete list on how God designed marriage, but it will definitely get us started.

In Genesis 2:18, God said, "It is not good that man should be alone." After God had created all the animals, both male and female, He realized Adam needed a counterpart as well. It was important to God that Adam not feel alone or lonely. "So the Lord God caused the man to fall into a deep sleep; and while he was sleeping, he took one of the man's ribs and then closed up the place with flesh. Then the Lord God made a woman from the rib he had taken out of the man, and he brought her to the man" (Genesis 2:21-22). Here is a fact, free of charge: man was created from dirt, but woman was created from bone. Genesis 2:18 continues to say, "I will make a helper comparable to him." Please note the woman was created to "help" or "complement" Adam, not stress him out. God's design of woman was for Adam to have a helper, the two becoming one working together. There is simply no negative connotation to God's plan here. His plan was a perfect and good plan and still is today! Over the years, society has tried to change this, but it simply will not work any other way than Gods way.

Genesis 2:25 states, "And they were both naked, the man and his wife, and were not ashamed." God's original design for marriage involved no need for covering of anything. One definition of naked is "bare, stripped." It is easy to recognize that this Scripture refers to physical nakedness, but nakedness also symbolizes the transparency required in our relationships—our vulnerability, both emotionally and spiritually. Our marriages should *always* be a safe place for husbands and wives.

Marriage God's way does not involve secrets of any sort. Full disclosure toward our spouses, openness, honesty, and integrity are required. In today's technological society, we might say that means full access to every password or I.D. that our spouses own. Many would baulk at this and say there is a trust issue. If God were here on earth today, He might say something along the lines of, "If you have nothing to hide, what is the problem?" Sad to say, many marriages are full of secrets today: secret credit cards, secret relationships, secret bank accounts, and secret addictions. Genesis 2:25 states they were "not ashamed." Any time full disclosure is not applied in our marriage relationships, shame will follow when the secret is exposed.

Interestingly, *Merriam-Webster's Collegiate Dictionary* defines shame as "a feeling of guilt, regret, or sadness that you have because *you know* you have done something wrong." Mom used to say, "It will all come out in the wash." Never quite understanding this as children, as we mature into adulthood, we have encountered enough lies to gain a full understanding of this statement. If you have ever washed clothes, you know that when the cycle starts to spin, it will walk its way from the wall if it is unbalanced, making loud noises, stopping, and making a buzzing sound for you to reset it. This is what happens in our relationships when a secret is discovered: the shocked spouses feel a spinning in their hearts and heads, they feel unbalanced, and they pull away from their spouses, making many sounds as they spin out of control. Their worlds have been rocked. If we think about it, God knew what He was doing to have them "naked." It is sin and our worldviews that change and distort this openness between husbands and wives. When we start to listen to the counsel of the world (e.g., "It's okay, he or she does not need to know that"), we slowly remove ourselves from God's design.

The Bible continues on to say, "When a man has taken a new wife, he shall not go out to war or be charged with any business; he shall be free at home one year, and bring happiness to his wife whom he has taken" (Deuteronomy 24:5). Wow! Many men might desire to get married for this reason alone. One full year of not working? Although we know in today's high-achieving, career-oriented world, this year off of work in order to bring happiness to our new brides will not cut it. However, God's design still stands. God intended for men to cherish their new brides and to bring them much happiness.

It was never God's design that once the ring is on and we are living in the same house with our new spouses, then the true us appears as we start to stop worrying about "getting the girl." Stated another way, if our dating process was all about impressing each other, we will most likely not recognize our spouses as time goes on and the *impressing* has stopped.

The first year of marriage is vital in building a strong foundation, to becoming one. The man was to recognize his new role as a husband as important. This role was to be placed at the top of his priority list. Today, we hear many women complain about the absence of their husbands in their homes due to work or outings with friends. In Ecclesiastes 9:9 we read, "Live joyfully with the wife whom you love all the days of your vain life which He has given you under the sun." Again, it is important to note that it was not God's plan for men to bring increased stress to their new brides, but much happiness and joy. We might add, this was and still must be an *intentional* act of bringing happiness and joy to their new brides. The same can be said for brides toward their new grooms. Many couples have suffered from the "bait and switch" concept in their marriages.

Dr. Emerson Eggerichs' book, *Love and Respect*, explains about a man's greatest need being "respect" and a woman's greatest need being "love" (Eggerichs, 2005). He basically states that women who do not feel loved by their husbands will not show respect toward their husbands, and men who do not feel respected by their wives will not show love toward their wives. Therefore, the relationship remains stalemated until one implements a change. Ephesians 5:33 states, "Nevertheless let each one of you in particular so love his own wife as himself, and let the wife see that she respects her husband." God designed the man to need respect and the woman to need love.

Consequently, when the Holy Spirit inspired the Apostle Paul to write the book of Ephesians, he deemed it necessary to include these needs in the Scriptures. Marriage relationships could soar to new levels if we would educate ourselves with God's design for marriage. We would save ourselves so much grief, strife, and pain simply by men *loving* their wives and women *respecting* their husbands. Sounds simple, but it takes conscience efforts on both parts to accomplish this.

Alright, the one you have been waiting for: 1 Corinthians 7:1-3 says, "Now for the matters you wrote about: 'It is good for a man not to have sexual relations with a woman. But since sexual immorality is occurring, each man should have sexual relations with his own wife, and each woman with her own husband. The husband should fulfill his marital duty to his wife, and likewise the wife to her husband" (NIV). Over time, we can definitely say our society has strayed from this design of God's. It is true that God, Himself, created sex. He created it for Adam and Eve to be fruitful and multiply and for pleasure. With this beautiful creation of sex, He set boundaries . . . It is for a marriage relationship **only**. It does not matter how hard you try to twist Scripture, there is simply no way around this design. Sex is for married couples only. God did not include "in love couples," "friends with benefits couples," "engaged couples," or any other type of relationship you can come up with. It really is a simple design.

Due to our lack of adhering to this design, much pain and suffering has occurred in our world. How many times have you listened to or heard about men or women who are devastated that their marriage vows were broken through affairs? How many times have you heard about pregnancies resulting from one-night-stands—and they do not know what to do? We will never know how many babies have been aborted because of the acts of sex outside of marriage. The list of tragedies can go on and on. Sex is definitely one of the many blessings of a marriage. God created both men and women with this desire of intimacy, so He provided them the perfect relationship in which this need is met.

It is also worth noting that sex is the *one* area that is solely limited in a relationship for marriage. In other relationships (parent and child, siblings, friendships, etc.), we extend honor, love, joy, and respect. These attributes are universal in various relationships. However, the act of sexual intimacy was created by God *only* for the covenant marriage between a man and a woman.

Hebrews 13:4 states, "Marriage should be honored by all" (NIV). What exactly does that mean? Let's start by defining the word honor. *Merriam-Webster's Collegiate*

Dictionary says that it is "a keen sense of ethical conduct: integrity; one's word given as a guarantee of performance; an evidence or symbol of distinction: an exalted title or rank."

We honor our marriages by thanking God for the blessing of our spouses, acknowledging that even with all their faults and failures, they are the "good and perfect" gift that God gave us. We honor our marriages by recognizing that God is the Designer and that without Him, we will not enjoy the full benefits of His beautiful design. We honor our marriages when we recognize that there are certain ethical conducts we are to exhibit as husbands and wives, toward each other and toward others. We honor our marriages when we hold integrity close to our hearts and understand the damage that happens when integrity is gone. We honor our marriages when we invite God to be the "head" of our marriage relationships.

Ecclesiastes 4:12 states, "Though one may be overpowered by another, two can withstand him. And a threefold cord is not quickly broken." God will be our sustaining power in our marriages if we include Him daily!

It is important that we understand there is a real enemy in this world that is out to destroy what God has given us. We need God's leadership in our marriages! Hebrews 13:4 continues to say, "And the marriage bed kept pure" (NIV). When we keep God's design for our marriage beds, we will not defile them. Anything outside of His design defiles our marriage beds. Our world today definitely views the marriage bed differently than God views the marriage bed. There is so much perverseness with sex today that many find God's design rigid. Despite the world's view, there is only one way that the marriage bed will have total fulfillment, and that is when it is honored, respected, and held sacred as God designed it.

Lastly, we honor our marriage relationships by allowing God to shape, form, and mold us to be the best spouses for our mates. As we honor our marriages by praying for our spouses and relationships daily, we will watch God bless our socks off and explode our marriages to the next level.

We have just scratched the surface of God's intent for our marriages. Generally, there are three types of couples: (1) those that know God's way and choose to go a different direction; (2) those who continue to pursue God's way and intentionally seek to adhere to it; and (3) those who are ignorant of God's design for marriage. Ignorance is simply a lack of knowledge, understanding, or education. Our divorce rate in society proves that many of us are either not following God's design for our marriage relationships or lacking knowledge of His perfect design. Each of us knows which category we fall into. Implementing changes in our marriages based on the few designs mentioned so far will propel our marriages into the blessing and beauty God intended.

If you have read to this point, you now have a portion

of God's design for a marriage relationship. We might say it is time to put the soap (education) in the washing machine (marriage relationship) and push start. Are you ready to do some laundry? It is time to receive EVERYTHING God intended for our marriages.

CHAPTER TWO

X-RAY

At age fifteen, I (Sissy) fell from approximately nine feet in the air onto a mat when dismounting the balance beam in gymnastics. Needless to say, an emergency room visit followed the fall. The doctors could not tell what was wrong with my back until they **X-RAYED** it. This x-ray provided the necessary images to diagnose that my back was broken in two spots. Most likely many are wondering, "What is the relevance of this story to marriage relationships?" Glad you asked that question.

Many of us have had an x-ray at some point in our lives. We know this is a diagnostic test to probe a little deeper into our problems to correctly assess what is causing our pains. Without this test, many times our issues are not able to be seen by the naked eye. We suggest it is a good idea to X-RAY our marriages every so often as well. In relationships, we will experience ups and downs. It is during the down times that an x-ray might be extremely helpful to get to the root of the pain. We are going to start with an x-ray of our minds (thoughts), then head straight to our hearts, and finish with our feet. Slip on your protective vest, and let's get started.

Philippians 2:5 says, "In your relationships with one another, have the same mindset as Christ Jesus" (NIV). As we dissect this verse, we first see that the Apostle Paul is speaking about relationships, which includes the marriage relationship. He goes on to state we are to have the mind of Christ. If we have no clue what Christ's mind was bent toward, how can we do this? Remember "Chapter One—Educate?" That's right; what does the Bible say about Christ's mind? As the chapter continues, Paul speaks of Christ's humility, how he came to serve and humble Himself. Here are a few questions we need to ask ourselves: "Am I humbling myself to my spouse?" "Am I serving my spouse?" "Am I keeping count on how many times I did this and believing that he or she has to catch up before I will serve again?"

These questions may seem trivial, but trust us when we say they are far from trivial. Many couples end up in extremely high maintenance relationships because they will not bend and serve their spouse. We are not to serve our spouses because they deserve it. Quite the contrary, we are to serve our spouses because we are to become Christ-like and have His mind. Simple. End of story. The Gospel is really quite simple as you can see. We try to make it more complicated and add all of our ifs, ands, or buts to justify our shortcomings. At the end of the chapter, we discover that God exalted Christ, not that Christ exalted Christ. We get so caught up in, "What about me? What about me?" that we forget God is the one who takes care of "me." Ask yourself: "Am I a servant-centered or self-centered mate?" Today is a great time to start being servants to our spouses—not begrudging servants, but ones who desire to serve because Jesus is working through us. We are not suggesting this is something that changes overnight. This act of becoming servant-centered will be a choice we make over and over again for many years to come.

Isn't this x-raying fun? Romans 12:2 says, "Do not conform to the pattern of this world, but be transformed by the renewing of your mind. Then you will be able to test and approve what God's will is—his good, pleasing, and perfect will" (NIV). As we look at the definition of conform in the *Merriam-Webster's Collegiate Dictionary*, we see it means "to behave according to socially acceptable conventions or standards." Obviously, if we conform to the ways of this world and its views of marriage, we will NEVER receive God's full benefits for our marriage relationships. It is simply not possible. God's benefits of marriage are directly related to His principles of pursuing marriage.

For example, we cannot plant apple seeds and plan on getting a fresh baked apple cobbler. There are several steps in between that must be fulfilled, and if we leave out the sugar (just one ingredient), the whole cobbler will have a different flavor. According to Romans 12:2, if we allow our minds to be transformed (renovated) with God's thoughts and plans, then and only then will we be able to achieve God's perfect will. Say a Believer marries a non-Believer—this is not in God's perfect will. Why? Because God does not desire for any of us to be unequally yoked, as it brings many more difficulties into our relationships (2 Corinthians 6:14). We still love God, but we *chose* to disobey His will; therefore, the relationship outcome is different. We may require more x-rays from an increase of pain in our relationships as a result of our disobedience (being unequally yoked). Remember, WE are responsible for our choices. We have walked in God's "permissive" will and we have walked in God's perfect will, and hands down, God's perfect will wins EVERY TIME! Do not beat yourself up if you are currently walking in God's "permissive" will. We have good news for you: it is never too late to begin pursuing God's purpose and plan for your marriage, His perfect will. When we sincerely repent, although the road may be rocky, God will lovingly guide us back to Him.

Before we finish x-raying our minds, let's look at another Scripture. For those of us who are Believers, this may sound really familiar. For those who might not consider ourselves Believers, this particular Scripture should enlighten you as to why some things just do not make sense in your relationships. "For we do not wrestle against flesh and blood, but against principalities, against powers, against the rulers of the darkness of this age, against spiritual hosts of wickedness in the heavenly places" (Ephesians 6:12).

We need to be honest with ourselves when we read this Scripture. It is so much easier to blame our spouses, whom we *can* see, than to blame some evil spiritual forces that we *cannot* see, right? When we are in a strong discussion, debate, heated conversation, whatever we like to term our fights, our minds are not focused on the evil forces at work at that particular moment. We are simply trying to figure out how we are going to respond next! Oh, how much peace could our marriage relationships enjoy if only we could focus our thoughts, anger, and energy as a team against these evil forces? Bottom line: just because we do not believe there are evil forces sent to destroy what God has planned for us does not mean they are not at work in our marriages. Although we cannot see the wind move the tree branches, we KNOW it is the wind that moves them back and forth. Do not question God's Word here. When He tells us evil forces are what we are wrestling with, we should believe Him. Why do we find it easier to believe that the men or women we fell in love with are the ones causing all of our pains rather than the evil forces? Pray against those forces attempting to take what God has given you.

Let's move the x-ray machine down to our hearts. The book of Proverbs has much to say about our hearts. We will start with a light verse. Proverbs 17:22 states, "A cheerful heart is good medicine, but a crushed spirit dries up the bones" (NIV). The world we live in is self-absorbed and contains various challenges, unrest, disharmony, and disrespect. The list could go on and on; however, you are breathing and living in this world, so you too are aware of our world's conditions. The adverse situations mentioned above are no respecter of persons. For example, when our economy is threatened, we all feel the effects. We might have different degrees of the effect, but bottom line is we all feel it. The Scripture above tells us that a "cheerful heart is good medicine."

How do we achieve a cheerful heart living in this world? The best and only sure way is to cling to God's Word and His promises. No matter what challenges we face today, in our marriages or anywhere else, God is *for us* and God is able to walk through it *with us!* First and foremost, face these challenges head on as a couple (one flesh) united with God as your Commanding General. Our marriages deserve both spouses pursuing a smooth and reliable relationship so our marriages do not add to life's stresses. We must make a point to be each other's encourager, cheerleader, sounding board, and covering. We need to lighten up in our day-to-day routines. We need to learn to laugh with each other. In our relationship, my husband is definitely the "clown" to lighten up a tough time. Understand there are many times that he does NOT try to be the clown; he simply has a way of making us both laugh. Thank God for His good medicine. There are unlimited refills on God's medicine and not one co-pay!

Many times it is hard for us to accept that *our* hearts could possibly be wicked. Wicked—that is such a harsh word. How about we use "deceitful" instead? Deceitful really does not sound any better, does it? However, Jeremiah 17:9 says, "The heart is deceitful above all things, and desperately wicked; who can know it?" For those of us who are fervently seeking God, we have a tendency to feel this verse is for someone else, but truly it is for ALL of us. Thank goodness for x-rays of our hearts; otherwise, we might not be able to recognize the need for a cleansing.

It is our assumption that most of us have had an iron in our hands at one time or another; if not, we will one day. The whole purpose of ironing is to smooth out all the wrinkles, and if we are really meticulous people, there will not be one wrinkle left when we finish. One of the most frustrating things about ironing is when we are just about finished and then, BAM! There it is, staring us in the face: a SPOT that we were unaware of. All our hard work of ironing is out the window because we cannot wear the shirt with the spot on it. This is how the deceit in our hearts works. Obviously, if we were aware that deceit was in our hearts, we would try really hard to remove it. However, what do we do when it is so deep inside our hearts that we simply cannot recognize it?

The Holy Spirit is the One who helps reveal such things to us. Romans 8:27, "Now He who searches the hearts knows what the mind of the Spirit is." Just as the iron must be heated to remove deeper wrinkles, the Holy Spirit convicts our hearts with "warmth" to press out the wrinkle of deceit. It is important to remember that sometimes when ironing, there are those stubborn wrinkles that take a little more pressure to remove. This is true with some of the areas of our hearts too. A heart full of corruptness in a marriage relationship will not prosper (Proverbs 17:20). We need to be willing to have our wrinkles removed from our hearts so our marriages can prosper to God's fullness.

When God created us, He made our hearts a very vital part of life. For example, if we were to receive no medical intervention when our hearts stop, we would die. So we do not have to be rocket scientists to understand that the health of our hearts is VITAL to our existence. It is also not surprising that God speaks to the health of the heart in the Bible frequently. The word "heart" appears some 830 times in the King James Version of the Bible. In marriage relationships, when we fall in love, our hearts are touched, which is a key factor. As time goes along, life starts to settle in, and we start to have struggles that did not exist when we first met. "Every way of a man is right in his own eyes, But the Lord weighs the hearts" (Proverbs 21:2). This verse may be part of the reason we disagree. Honestly, there is not one of us who does not think that what we believe or feel is correct; otherwise, we would not put our opinions out there on the table. The question we must ask is: "Does what we believe or feel line up with what God says about such matters?" How many times have we known ourselves or other couples to defend to the end their opinions, no matter what damage it does to our marital relationships? Again, we go back to God's design. If we have God as the head of our relationships, then God is the deciding factor in the dispute. Much easier said than played out.

This is why God says in Proverbs 4:23, "Above all else, guard your heart, for everything you do flows from it" (NIV). Our hearts can be influenced so quickly and easily by this world. If we are desiring to receive the fullness of God's beautiful design for our marriage relationships, we must protect our hearts from the influence of the ways of this world. In order for us to have uniquely blessed marriages, we must do things differently. Doing things God's way means we humble ourselves. So what if we are right? We must learn to turn our hearts to God and trust Him to handle things His way.

The other day while driving, we had a green light and started to proceed toward the intersection. We have learned to look first because of accidents we have witnessed. Thank

God we looked! As we were starting to head out, a black blur flew past as a car ran the red light. Although we were completely right in driving into the intersection because we had a green light, we could have endured a serious accident. At the end of the day, we must ask ourselves: "Is my rightness worth the destruction it can bring into my relationship?"

We have x-rayed our minds and our hearts. Now for our feet. Although we may not think about it often, our feet are an important part of our bodies. Our feet are the very foundation of what holds us up. It has been said many times, "When a man has large feet, he has a good foundation." As we x-ray our feet, we can see the paths they choose to travel.

"Ponder the path of your feet, and let all your ways be established" (Proverbs 4:26). It is clear to see that our Creator knew that our feet could get us into trouble, so He instructs us to think about what path we are allowing our feet to travel. Often, many troubles could have been avoided had we thought about the route we were on. How many times have you heard something along the lines of, "Boy, I wish I would have never gone there." Some of us might be thinking that very thought right now.

A path is most commonly known as a route or course that one travels. However, *Merriam-Webster's Collegiate Dictionary* gives another definition: "a way of life, conduct, or thought." There is a strong correlation between the paths we choose to travel in life and our behaviors that follow. For example, when we were younger, we may have decided to go to a party that involved things we really did not want to partake in. If we traveled the route anyway and arrived at the party, we placed ourselves in a position in which our behaviors, thoughts, and ways of life could be tempted to adapt to our surroundings.

Especially as a married couple, we must be intentional about where we allow our feet to take us. Slow down and listen to the still small voice that says, "You do not really want to go there, do you?" Many relationships have suffered greatly after the wrong paths have been traveled by our spouses. It is important to make sure our feet go where and only where we know God is welcomed and comfortable. After all, He is with us wherever we go!

Living in this world provides a wide selection of paths for all of us to follow. One may say it is too hard to avoid the wrong path ALL the time. However, in the Bible, Proverbs 3:6 says, "In all your ways acknowledge Him, and He shall direct your paths." God has provided a way of help for us to keep our paths straight; we simply need to be obedient and submit to Him! What exactly does this submission look like? It is interesting that one definition *Merriam-Webster's Collegiate Dictionary* gives for submission is: "to stop trying to fight or resist something: to agree to do or accept something that you have been resisting or opposing." Therefore, using this definition, God is asking us to follow His principles and to stop resisting and opposing Him.

We must not forget God is the Designer of marriage. If the Designer says in His handbook, the Bible, to submit and He will make our paths straight, we are really asking for trouble if we detour. God did not design marriage to fail. That would be absurd. He designed marriage to flourish and be fulfilling. God knows how challenging the world we live in can be. He knows the temptations that are lurking to trap us and destroy our relationships. This is why God's design for us is to stay close to Him. He will not lead us astray. When people are asked to perform a "walk the line" test for drunkenness while driving, it is their hope that they walk a straight line. If not, they are most likely going to jail. It is our wish that our desire to avoid jail (become a prisoner of our own steps) is stronger than our desire to veer off the path God designed for us.

One of the most important reasons to cautiously place our feet is found in Psalm 1:1. This Scripture states, "Blessed is the one who does not walk in step with the wicked or stand in the way that sinners take or sit in the company of mockers" (NIV). It is clear to see in this verse that traveling down a winding road outside of God's path is where the wicked travel. The choice is ours. Do we want to step with the wicked and receive their rewards, or do we want to walk the path God designed and receive His blessings? This walk in our relationships must be a smooth walk as if were are waltzing down the road. In a waltz, we must keep rhythm with the beat of one-two-three, one-two-three for a smooth dance. We both must go down-up-up, down-up-up with our one-two-three count; otherwise, we will not appear as one, but as two individuals who are bobbing up and down like fishing corks. We certainly do not want our marriage relationships to bob up and down. During those down times, we have the potential to be swallowed by a big fish and not bounce back up. We want to avoid those fish out there and learn where our feet should and should not go.

We are aware of the many areas of our marriages we can and should x-ray. However, we just wanted to achieve a jump start and share the need to periodically dig deeper in our relationships. Any significant relationship—whether spousal, parent-child, sibling, etc.—is going to require sacrifice and effort, but the return on the investment is beyond measure. The popular saying, "You are what you eat," can be compared to our relationships as well. We will get back from our relationships exactly what we put into them. Many times our pains are so deep that we cannot discover why we react or respond the way we do without a deeper probing. Thank goodness God has provided us the oldest most reliable x-ray machine around, the Holy Spirit!

CHAPTER THREE

PURSUE

Most of us are familiar with the phrase, "in hot pursuit." Let's take a minute and remember back to when we were in "hot pursuit" of our mates. It is good for us to reminisce about the early days of our relationships. Many of us wonder, "How in the world did we function on such little sleep?" As great as it is to remember those "hot pursuit" days, it is harmful to our relationships when we STOP the pursuit of our mates.

The word "**PURSUE**" is used in the Bible to guide us in several areas of our lives. When we pursue something, we take an action toward something. Remember the first time we fell in love or thought we were in love? We spent every waking minute thinking about that person. We called him or her all hours of the day. For those of you who are a bit younger, texting back and forth all day long is more likely. Our goal was to make sure the other party knew we thought something was special about them. In order to get this point across, we had to pursue, or take action toward, that person. We did not need a sticky note reminding us, "Make sure you call or text so-and-so." Why? Simply because our hearts were in it. It was something we desired, and we were going to make it happen. We were in pursuit!

What about when we pursue a job? Once we have a job, it definitely is to our advantage not to take it for granted, especially if the economic climate is unstable. If we have only been employed with a company for a few months or we are neck and neck with another co-worker for a promotion, our pursuit is most likely at its peak, well over 100 percent. Because we are in pursuit, we do not need someone to remind us to put our best feet forward or work hard. We know the type of impression we want to make, and we go after it. One might be asking, "Doesn't the Lord want us to pursue our jobs with much vigor and effort?" After all, Colossians 3:23 states, "Whatever you do, work it with all your heart as working for the Lord and not human masters" (NIV). Of course He does. Most of us do not have a problem pursuing those things important to **us**; we just need to make sure our greatest pursuits are our relationships with God, which is **His desire!**

Proverbs 15:9 states, "But he loves one who pursues

righteousness" (NIV). Since we know we are to pursue righteousness, what exactly is righteousness? The simplest way to describe righteousness is to say we are to pursue the character of Christ and desire holiness. Yes, this is simple to say, but it's more difficult to put into action day after day after day. How are we to attain the image of Christ in our everyday lives? First, there is absolutely no way this can be accomplished without having a humble heart. We must recognize that we need Christ's character in our lives. Once we are pursuing His righteousness, we will be better equipped to pursue the other things in our lives that matter to us, such as our spouses or significant others. Christ's character *in us* is key to pursing a strong, beautiful marriage relationship.

Most of us would agree that when we dated, it was natural for us to pursue each other. As time goes on, what happens to our pursuits? Many times it starts to lessen because life happens. We do not *intentionally* stop pursuing our mates; we are just trying to keep all things in order. We think to ourselves, "If the pursuit of this relationship slows a bit, so be it."

The problem with this thinking is that there is a price that will be paid, and our relationships will reap the consequences from this lack of pursuit. God wants us to pursue with our whole hearts excellence in our marriage relationships. Possibly we have heard friends, co-workers, or even family members share after a period of time in their marriages that they feel emotionally, mentally, and physically drained. Over time, they have come to view their mates as "regular or sub-par" males or females and to think that "the thrill is gone." They start to become less attracted to their spouses and no longer believe they have anything in common. So the next logical thing to do is to dispose of these relationships and find new exciting ones.

The challenge comes when we expect relationships equivalent or even better than when we proactively pursued our mates but we are no longer putting the effort into creating these types of relationships. We MUST always be intentionally pursuing our mates! There are many times we may not be so attractive to Christ with some of our attitudes, mannerisms, words, or actions. In those times, need we continue? We are so glad Jesus does not quit on any of us. He continues to extend love and grace, helping us through with the Holy Spirit to get back on track. 1 Timothy 6:11 says, "But you, O man of God, flee these things and pursue righteousness, godliness, faith, love, patience, gentleness." Jesus never tells us to stop pursuing our mates when we are tired, angry, or any other feelings we are experiencing.

"Let him turn away from evil and do good; let him seek peace and pursue it" (1 Peter 3:11). A marriage that has peace will last. There is not one man or woman who desires a life of utter chaos! If we will allow the Lord to change our hearts and spirits through prayer, the Holy Spirit will give us power to make exciting, drastic changes in our lives. As we follow His leading, attraction and anything else lacking will come back in full measure. Remember, marriage only works as God designed it. Trying to make marriage work any other way will not lead to receiving its full benefits!

As our relationships continue over time, we often forget about what it took to "get the girl or get the boy." If we will keep our eyes focused on the Designer's plan for our marriages, we will walk through our relationships much easier. We must always remember there is a real enemy out to sabotage what God has so beautifully designed. Satan cannot stand marriage. After all, our churches today are made up of families, and families are started with a man and a woman marrying. John 10:10 says, "The thief does not come except to steal, and to kill, and to destroy. I have come that they may have life, and that they may have it more abundantly."

If Satan recognizes that God designed marriage, we better wake up and realize we need to be pursuing God like never before. We cannot effectively handle all of our mates' imperfections, insecurities, and emotional ups and downs that come with life without actively pursuing the image of Christ. It is through our nature becoming like His nature that we will have the desire to continue to pursue one another.

Think about that very special shirt that was purchased with such excitement. When we first washed it, we took special care of it. We started out by hand washing it. As time went on, we put it in the washing machine on delicate cycle by itself. Now, we just throw it in with the rest of our clothes. All of a sudden, we notice that it has lost some of its color and shine. Now that we just toss it in with other items, it has those little annoying, rolled-up balls that make it not so special any longer. We definitely do not want our marriages to start having rolled-up balls popping up every-where. We want them to shine and be fresh for the many years ahead, so we must treat these relationships as extra special. We must never stop pursuing God or our mates!

CHAPTER FOUR

LOVE

How many of you have heard, "I love you, but I am not in love with you?" Believe it or not, this is a common phrase when breaking the news of an upcoming divorce to a spouse. This once "in love" couple has now become a "not in love with you" couple. How does this happen?

Could it be that the word **"LOVE"** contains such a powerful meaning, but oftentimes it is tossed around as a commonplace word when not knowing the full Biblical meaning of the word? Perhaps after a first date with a wonderful man, we find ourselves thinking things like, "I *love* the way he treated me. He opened my door and paid for the dinner; he was so attentive." The word "love" in this context cannot be a love that will last throughout a marriage relationship. Many of us "love" Mexican food or a great movie, but we need to know that "love" for our marriage relationships will only last if used and given in the context the Creator intended.

In Mark 12:30, Christ's first commandment to us is: "And you shall love the Lord your God with all your heart, with all your soul, with all your mind, and with all your strength." The Lord wants us to love Him *first* with our whole beings, yes, before we can begin to love anyone else. The conflict today is we misuse this Biblical word called "love." We must first remember "for God is love" (1 John 4:8). Most of us have it backwards. Many of us when dating tend to first fall in love with our dates, and we believe later on we can individually or collectively love God as our relationships progress. This is not the Lord's design for a Biblically-based, lasting relationship for a man and a woman. This is a superficial love, and it will not endure the trials of life.

Some of us may have lived in the 1970s or may enjoy listening to "oldies, but goodies" music. Therefore, we are most likely familiar with the 1975 hit song by Captain and Tennille titled, "Love Will Keep Us Together." One line of the lyrics is, "Love, love will keep us together. Think of me babe whenever some sweet-talking girl comes along, singing her song."

Let's pause and ask ourselves, "Will our love, on its own, be strong enough to love our spouses in the midst of life's trials?" When "some sweet-talking girl comes along?" What about when one of us erupts in anger because our basic needs are not being met for a few days, weeks, months, or even years? Will our own love, without Christ, be enough to continue to be joyful and happy in our relationships amid the challenges that we will all face during our lifetimes? There will be times we simply do not *feel* our spouses' love, and we *feel* we have been let down and defeated by the ones we love. Friends, only the love that Christ provides can rescue us from our own selfish love that focuses on me, me, me. If we attempt to love our spouses according to our feelings, we will be all over the map. Our feelings can change in a blink of an eye.

So the question arises: "What other love is there than our own love?" Is there a love that can truly keep us together? Our Lord says through the Apostle Paul in 1 Corinthians 13:4-7, "Love is patient, love is kind. It does not envy, it does not boast, it is not proud. It does not dishonor others, it is not self-seeking, it is not easily angered, and it keeps no record of wrongs. Love does not delight in evil but rejoices with the truth. It always protects, always trusts, always hopes, always perseveres" (NIV). Wow, that is a tall order! There is no way any of us can accomplish this type of love without the help of the Holy Spirit. Remember: God IS LOVE!

In order for us to really understand the power of how our Lord wants us to love each other, it is imperative we embrace the Scripture above. To truly comprehend and know how to love someone, it is important to have one of God's love ingredients: patience! The world we live in today is polar opposite of patient. Email and other great technological advances have created a society that wants what they ask for *right now*. This includes love as well! The prospect of waiting on anything is not popular! Especially when we see everyone with someone by their side.

As the farmer plants a seed in fertile soil, he may wish there would be leaves quickly sprouting up out of the dirt in a few days; however, in reality, it takes much longer. The seeds must be watered, fertilized, and protected before there is any noticeable produce on top of the dirt. Waiting on God in situations such as choosing a mate or finding that next job should involve patience. Patience is a virtue and gift that God gives us to protect us, a type of insurance policy if you will, from making bad decisions in our lives. True patience is only acquired when we seek it through prayer. As our patience grows, we can rest assured that we are maturing in our relationships with God. It is His strength that will equip us to exhibit patience in diverse situations. The Lord loves it when we are patiently waiting on Him.

At the same time, He wants us to take action and then allow His blessings to flow in His timing. For example, we do not want the love in our relationships to be heated by the fast-working microwave ovens. As many of us have experienced, once you microwave something, it is very hot, but it loses so much of its flavor, and the texture changes. Let's not forget it cools really fast too. Think about sliding a nice, thick, long piece of bacon into the microwave. Without a doubt, when you pull it out of the microwave, it looks different, curled up half the size.

Now take that same piece of bacon and let it cook slowly over the stove. Your bacon looks and tastes much better. God did not intend our love to heat up rapidly in marriage, lose flavor, and fizzle out quickly. We cheat ourselves when we do not follow His design and do not wait patiently for a love that is slow-cooked over a long period of time with great results at the end. Oh, the flavor simply cannot be beat!

Another ingredient the Lord wants us to grasp is kindness. When everyday stresses of life seem to push us to the edge or maybe even push us over the edge, and anger flares up, we are still supposed to express kindness. As we are patient with each other, the Lord naturally brings out our kindness. *Merriam-Webster's Collegiate Dictionary* defines kindness as "having or showing a gentle nature and desire to help others." Interestingly enough, parts of this definition are words Christ might have used: "being gentle with others and the desire to help others." The challenge we all face is how to continue to be gentle to people who are, quite frankly, not so gentle to us. We all encounter those times when we have a hard day at work or wherever, and the last thing we feel like doing is being kind to our spouses, especially on a day when their attitude may be less than spectacular. We simply are spent by the time we make it home. We truly just want to be alone. We need to remember Jesus displayed great kindness, gentleness, and joyfulness that never wavered due to his emotions. Without the help of the Holy Spirit, we are left to our own sinful natures, full of our own selfish desires that fall short of God's desire for us. A lasting marriage relationship will be one in which each spouse chooses to be kind, especially when we do not feel or think our spouses are deserving of our kindness in that moment. God's love working through us is not about what we deserve; it is about what we are willing to give!

Another character trait of love is that the Lord does not want us to be full of envy of others' lives and possessions. Envy is defined in *Merriam-Webster's Dictionary* as "the feeling of wanting to have what someone else has." As we dissect this definition, let us look at the word "feeling." The Lord gave us feelings and emotions that make up our personalities, but if we are to make our important decisions based on our feelings only, what a MESS! As stated earlier, it is highly likely our feelings will change the next day, by hours or even minutes. When we allow envy of someone else's possessions or life to take place in our hearts, we cannot activate the Lord's power of love in our own lives.

One way to help prevent envy from taking root in our hearts is to always remember that we only see what happens on the outside of relationships, and we only know what is shared about those relationships. Every couple has their own struggles to work through. The old saying that "the grass is greener on the other side of the fence" has sent many couples down a wrong pathway in their relationships.

Oftentimes, harboring envy implies that we do not yet understand and appreciate that God has created us as unique individuals with purposes and plans for our lives accordingly. Each of us are in various seasons when it comes to our growth in the Lord. Another familiar saying is, "Don't want for what someone else has unless you are willing to do what it took for them to get it." Our walks with God are processes, and we must walk out our specific plans. Instead of letting envy come into our hearts, we should be encouraged when we see God blessing others who may have already arrived at the season we are striving toward.

Jeremiah 9:23 says, "Let not the wise boast of their wisdom or the strong boast of their strength or the rich boast of riches, but let the one boast about this that they have the understanding to know me that I am the Lord" (NIV). The Lord says love does not boast. In general, men, more so than women, share their accomplishments with anyone who will listen. Regardless if you are wise, strong, or rich, God tells us not to boast.

Many relationships are started with sharing about each other's accomplishments, trying to "impress" one another.

Early on in the relationship this might be acceptable because you are getting to know each other. However, one can quickly decipher whether they have encountered a bragging person or a person simply sharing previous endeavors. Most of us would agree that we are not attracted to a "know-it-all" or an egotistical individual, male or female. God's design was for us to always remember that He is our source of all good! We cannot love our mates when we are consumed with ourselves and our achievements. This is simply selfish, and we will deteriorate our relationships quickly.

God's design of love is serving others and humbling ourselves. Philippians 2:3 says, "Do nothing out of rivalry or conceit, but in humility consider others as more important than yourselves" (HSCB). We are to encourage and inspire our spouses, not compete with them or remind them how wonderful we are. A constant diet of "look at me" is not the love that God gives us. This type of love will never last without a resenting spouse on the other end of it. Each of us has a choice to be a humble spouse cheering on our spouses to their full potentials or the boastful spouse sucking all the air out of our relationships. Which will you choose?

God's design of love also safeguards us from an angry spirit, and it does not keep a record of wrongs. Although God gave us our emotions like joy, sadness, and anger, Ephesians 4:26-27 states, "Be angry and do not sin, do not let the sun go down on your wrath, nor give place to the devil." Now, if we are to be honest, most of us at one time or another have gone to bed angry with our spouses. You know, the kind of anger that draws a very obvious line in the middle of the bed. The type of anger where you are almost falling off the side of the bed because you want to make sure your spouse cannot touch you. You want your spouse to *know* you are angry. As we look back at that, how silly are we? This Scripture we just mentioned tells us not to give Satan any opportunity. This means when we go to bed with anger in our hearts, Satan is now free to affect our spirits during our sleep. He tells us all kinds of lies in the night, we wake up believing them, and guess what? Our anger and fighting most likely continue, sometimes with greater intensity.

God's design for us to love does not involve unresolved anger. We cannot be angry and unforgiving and have communion with God at the same time. Have you ever tried to pray when you are angry with your spouse? Talk about a really difficult prayer. It is impossible! We must extend grace and forgiveness to our spouses. Understand this does not mean the actions or words possibly spoken are right; it simply means we *choose* to not allow bitterness to grow like an uncontrollable mold in our homes! Allowing our anger to control us is like taking a load of clothes out of the dryer and leaving them on the couch for a few days. It is almost impossible to smooth the wrinkles out with our hands. It will take an iron or another round in the dryer. Again, it is okay to become angry, but not okay for anger to overcome us and keep us immersed in it all night long and for days thereafter!

Prayerfully, after reading this chapter on love, we will consider thinking twice before using this Biblical word carelessly. Rather, we need to be intentional when we use the word "love" and should avoid casual use of this word or at least be able to recognize the differences. We should strive hard to make sure the next person we say "I love you" to is the person we want to: (1) extend much patience to, (2) exhibit extreme kindness to, (3) think more highly of them than ourselves, (4) walk in confidence and not envy, (5) boast about God and them and not ourselves, and (6) resolve our anger before the sun goes down.

God's design for marriage certainly includes His love, which is "agape" love. This is unconditional love, and we can only love unconditionally if we are led by the Holy Spirit. Agape love is the ONLY love that does not hinge on our emotions. This love is regardless of how we feel. Our mates will disappoint us; they will anger us; they may not be kind on certain days, but we are to love them unconditionally just as God has loved us. The world will encourage us to get even and lead us down very destructive pathways for our relationships. This should not surprise any of us. God is the creator of marriage, not anyone else!

When we choose to love our spouses the way God

designed, our relationships will be set on a path of *true* love. This is only accomplished through a constant intentional cleansing of ourselves with God in prayer. Think about the fact that we wash our clothes more than once. We do not depend on the one wash cycle to keep them clean from then on out. No, we wash them routinely to keep them fresh and clean. In the same manner, we must continue to be washed in God's love daily so we can extend His unconditional love to our mates daily.

CHAPTER FIVE

OPERATE

As we continue to explode our relationships, we want to look at the word **"OPERATE."** We have discussed **E**ducate, **X**-ray, **P**ursue, and **L**ove, and now we want to look at how we **O**perate. Many times when we hear the word "operate" we think of a surgeon operating on some part of our bodies or someone else's body. Today, we want to look at "operate" as the manner in which we control or function in our marriages. Is the Holy Spirit operating (controlling or functioning) in our everyday relationships? The Holy Spirit's operation in our lives can be compared to the washing machine temperature: cold, warm, or hot! Let's look a little closer and see at what temperature the Holy Spirit is functioning in our marriage relationships.

Romans 12:6-8 states, "We have different gifts, according to the grace given to each of us. If your gift is prophesying, then prophesy in accordance with your faith; if it is serving, then serve; if it is teaching, then teach; if it is to encourage, then give encouragement; if it is giving, then give generously; if it is to lead, do it diligently; if it is to show mercy, do it cheerfully" (NIV). It is important to take note that these items mentioned earlier are gifts. If we purchased a gift for a couple, offered it to them, and they never opened and used the gift, then of course the gift is of no benefit to the couple. This is true of our gifts from the Holy Spirit as well. We are going to unwrap three of these gifts: (1) service, (2) encouragement and (3) mercy. We could also look at the gifts of giving and leading in our relationships as well, but for now we will examine and focus on these three gifts.

Honestly, how many of us, when we fell in love and got engaged, thought how excited we were that now we have the greatest serving opportunities ever? Most likely not many of us. More likely, we thought, "Marriage will be amazing, and he or she will take care of all my needs. He or she is so kind, loving, and compassionate—everything I ever dreamed of." Not long after we return from our honeymoons, everyday life starts to transpire. Many times relationships start to take on different tones. Please do not confuse this as we should not have become married! Quite the contrary, it simply means we are now needing to learn to become "one." A verse in the Bible many seem to just read over is when Jesus said, "For even the Son of Man did not come to be served, but to serve, and to give His life a ransom for many" (Mark 10:45). Why would Jesus leave his beautiful position of authority in Heaven to come and serve? A great many of us have a hard time understanding the King of Kings and Lord of Lords as serving others. Aren't these positions ones of royalty in which many serve the authority figure? Regardless of our lack of understanding, this is exactly what Jesus did.

As Believers, after our salvation we are to strive to be more and more like Christ. Believe it or not, this includes serving others and our spouses, which in turn means we are serving Christ Jesus. Society today has a much different view. Its more common view is, "We are put here to be served, and, might we add, if you do not serve in the way we like, we will let you know it so you can get it right next time." Why do you think we find it so hard to serve when one of the gifts from the Holy Spirit is serving? Possibly we have not tapped into the right "temperature" of the operation of the Holy Spirit in our lives.

As we continue to look at serving our spouses, it is very important that we recognize that serving is not optional as some might think. We are to be imitators of Christ, and He said Himself, "Son of Man did not come to be served, but to serve." Our marriage relationships are the greatest opportunities to serve another individual, namely our spouses. We live with our spouses; we see the good, the bad, and the ugly, AND we are still instructed to serve our spouses. These gifts were not given to any of us to use ONLY IF someone serves you or ONLY IF someone is ALWAYS thinking of us first.

Serving our spouses takes conscious, intentional efforts. Although the majority of us are quite comfortable being served, it is going against our inborn natures to serve. Let's face it: we have worked hard all day, and when we get home, it is OUR time. Can we share a little secret? There is a supernatural principle working here; the more we serve our spouses, the more our spouses will start to reciprocate, and the closer we are to receiving the beautiful benefits of marriage that our Designer intended for us. Some questions we might ask ourselves are: (1) "Am I willing to go against my selfish nature and serve as the Designer of marriage has suggested?" (2) "Is my marriage relationship important enough to follow the Designer's plan and forget about the societal norm?" (3) "Are we serving one another in the same manner we want to be served?" and (4) "Are we pleased with our relationships as they are currently, or do we want to EXPLODE our relationships?" When we set our relationships on the "hot" temperature setting with the Holy Spirit, we can be assured the Holy Spirit is ready to start the cleaning process!

Now we would like to examine the gift of encouraging. Many of us would agree that life today can be brutal. All one has to do is walk outside the door, get in the car, and watch the "encouragement" of fellow drivers. Right? Not hardly. It is more like, "Get out of my way, or I may blow you away!" We live in such a fast-paced, high-achieving, and "me"-centered society that most human beings do not have time nor the thought processes to consider others. After all, they are simply trying to keep it all together and look like life is perfect. We all need some encouragement every now and then. When we encourage our spouses, we are bringing hope to them; we are speaking confidence into them, and we are providing support for them. These are basic needs we all desire and, quite frankly, need in our lives. We get beat up enough in this world outside our homes. The last place we need to receive more of this treatment is inside the walls of our homes. So are we allowing the gift of encouraging to flow through us to our mates?

The Designer of marriage, God, knew we all needed encouragement. As married couples, it is ideal that we have each other to encourage one another. Again, the Holy Spirit gives us the gift of encouraging, and in addition to this, God tells us to encourage one another. Ecclesiastes 4:9-10 states, "Two are better than one, because they have a good return for their labor: For if they fall, one will lift up his companion. But woe to him who is alone when he falls, for he has no one to help him up." All of us are going to need help up at one point or another in our lives. Our goal as married couples is to become one flesh. When our spouses are down, we are encouraging ourselves as well as our spouses as we stretch out our hands to lift them up. We are not supposed to watch our mates fall and leave them there while we tend to our own business. The Scripture we just read suggests that when our spouses fall, we help them up regardless of how we feel, regardless if they are part of the reason they fell—regardless of anything!

"My goal is that they may be encouraged in heart and united in love, so that they may have the full riches of complete understanding, in order that they may know the mystery of God, namely, Christ" (Colossians 2:2) (NIV). As this Scripture states, when we encourage our spouses, we also have the benefit of becoming united in love and having the ability for "complete understanding" of the "mystery of God." There will be those times that we are pressed hard for the words or actions to encourage our spouses, and that is precisely when the Holy Spirit comes in, as long as we allow Him to operate to His full potential in our lives. He will give us the words, the actions, and the proper timing if He is allowed to be in control. Oh no, the "c" word: control. Yes, we are going to have to surrender control to the Holy Spirit and let Him put His spin on our marriages. Going back to the laundry, we might say encouraging our spouses is comparable to the starch we use to iron a shirt. This starch builds up the material to hold it in place better and prevent wrinkles so easily. Our encouragement for our spouses builds them up to walk out into the world with their heads held high and know that they are not alone in these challenging times.

One last thought on encouraging our mates. It is important to note that encouraging our spouses also helps them resist sin. When we are down, lose hope, or feel there is no answer to our problems, it is much easier for the enemy to lie and deceive us. "But encourage one another daily, as long as it is called 'today,' so that none of you may be hardened by sin's deceitfulness" Hebrews 3:13 (NIV). It is important to note that encouraging each other in our marriage relationships is not only for when we are down; it is a *daily* privilege to encourage each other. After all, we married these men and women because we saw some wonderful qualities and traits in them. Years after the "I do's" are said, it is even more important to remind each other of these great qualities. When we wash a load of dirty clothes after yardwork, if we open the lid after the water has filled the machine, we most likely will see muddy, murky water from the dirt and filth of the day's work. We do not want to let the dirt, filth, and muddy waters of this life leave permanent stains in our relationships. We need to make it a point to accept the gift of encouragement from the Holy Spirit and encourage our mates daily. Matter of fact, more than once a day is even better!

Let us look at the gift of mercy now. As children we used to play a game called "Mercy." Some of us may or may not have played this game. In this game, you clasp hands with each other while facing one another. When you say "go," both parties start applying pressure to the other's hand to bend their fingers back. It is not until one person yells, "Mercy!" that the other person stops applying pressure. Granted, this may not sound like a fun game, but surprisingly, many girls and boys have at one time or another participated in this game called "Mercy." The whole point to this game is that one person controls whether or not to release the other person when they scream, "Mercy!"

The word "mercy" can be described as: "Compassion or forgiveness shown toward someone whom it is within one's power to punish or harm." Again, the Holy Spirit offers us the gift of "mercy." Obviously, Jesus is the greatest example of mercy one will ever find. His mercies are new every morning (Lamentations 3:23). Over and over again, He extends mercy to each of us. Why do we find it so hard to extend mercy to someone we love dearly and are united with as one? It all goes back to our selfish sinful natures. It is natural to reciprocate what has been done to us.

For example, we talked about encouraging one another. If we are encouraged, we are more likely to encourage the one who encouraged us. If our spouses serve us, we are more likely to serve them back. This is also true if our spouses lash out at us; we are more likely to lash back. We must make a cognizant effort to extend mercy to our spouses. This mercy does not come naturally to most people. We might say extending mercy to our spouses is like adding fabric softener to our washes. It softens the roughness of the load. Mercy is the first step in softening your relationship in a heated discussion, and it freshens the mood!

Truly the Holy Spirit needs full operating authority in this area of mercy. We should let Him work through us to extend mercy to our spouses. Matthew 5:7 says, "Blessed are the merciful, for they shall obtain mercy." In the Beatitudes (Matthew 5:3-7), Jesus states that the merciful are blessed. This Scripture also talks about receiving mercy when extending mercy. This is a simple sowing and reaping process. If we extend mercy, we will be more likely to receive mercy. Mercy can also be defined as receiving something you do NOT deserve!

This is precisely what each of us receives when we accept Christ as our Lord and Savior. We did not deserve Jesus to take on ALL of OUR sins, but yet He did. Who are we to imitate? Yes, Jesus Christ! The next time our spouses offend us, we need to try putting on our "Jesus Superhero" costumes and extend mercy! That's right: let the Holy Spirit's power flow through us and function in a capacity that is undeniably full of MERCY! Inevitably, it will not be long until each of us will need mercy extended back to us.

We go back to the washing machine . . . It goes something like this: fill the tub with water, wash clothes, rinse, spin. Our marriage relationships are similar to this: offend our spouses, apologize, ask for forgiveness, forgiveness is extended, and we are ready for the next cycle. Unfortunately, when we do not extend mercy, we clog up our relationships with bitterness, anger, and resentment, and we are no longer able to have a healthy wash cycle! It is not a matter of *if* we are going to need mercy extended to us; it truly is a matter of *when* we are going to need mercy extended to us.

Obviously, how we OPERATE in our marriage relationships is dependent upon what or who is controlling our relationships. The Designer of marriage wants the total operation of our relationships dependent upon the power in which the Holy Spirit extends to us. Marriage was designed to be a wonderful relationship with so many benefits attached. As married couples allowing the Holy Spirit to function fully in our relationships, we will enjoy being served, encouraged, and extended mercy when we truly do not deserve any of it. This is the type of relationship that will stand the trials of this life!

CHAPTER SIX

DESIGN

Let's move right along into **DESIGN**. As we have mentioned several times throughout this book, God is the Designer of marriage. First, let's look at the definition of the word design. *Merriam-Webster's Collegiate Dictionary* states that design is "to plan and make (something) for a specific use or purpose." God definitely has specific uses and purposes for our marriages. Unfortunately, our world has completely distorted that original use and purpose today.

We love the Scripture in Jeremiah 29:11: "'For I know the plans I have for you,' declares the Lord, 'plans to prosper you and not to harm you, plans to give you hope and a future'" (NIV). This Scripture is true for each of us

55

individually and for each married couple. Think about the assurance we can walk in if we will simply believe what God says!

Although life can be tough and marriage takes work, not one of the challenges any of us face will go unused for God's plans for us. Romans 8:28 says, "And we know that all things work together for good to those who love God, to those who are the called according to His purpose." A very important part of this verse is "to those who love him." Many times this verse is quoted only in part, and people end up confused as to why things have not worked together for their good. If we do not confess love for God and act upon that confession, this verse will not apply to us. Please don't kill the messengers here; we are just quoting God's Word.

As we examine God's design, we see He first of all has plans for us. One question we might want to ask ourselves as married couples is, "Do we ourselves have plans for our relationships?" This might seem a bit elementary to some, but it might come as a surprise to know how many couples honestly have not thought out plans for their relationships. Many fly by the seat of their pants on a day-to-day basis. Couples handling marriage this way are pretty easy to spot. Their relationships are up and down and up and down and up and down. Before too long, there is very little up, and mostly down is the direction they head! It would make sense that if the Designer of marriage designed it with plans, then we too might need to implement some sort of plans to our marriage relationships. A good place to start would be the Designer's plans!

Next, we see that not only does God have plans, but they are plans to prosper us and not harm us. This should make all of us excited! When most people hear the word "prosper" they instantly think of their pocketbook. God's design goes far beyond our pocket books. Yes, He designed us to prosper financially, but that does not mean that we are all going to be millionaires! He also designed us to prosper in health, physically and mentally, to live in peace and joy. As a married couple, living in peace is something most want more than money. Let's face it: we can have all the money in the world and live in total chaos, volatility, and disgruntlement, and that money will not fix any of it. On the other hand, we have seen and have experienced ourselves peace when finances are stretched to the limit. Hands down, we desire the Creator's design of peace over rolling in the dough any day! Peace is what we need when our spouses are laid off or when the doctor brings a bad report or when our children go astray.

What about prospering with a Godly mate? Going through this world with a Godly man or woman by our sides is definitely prospering. Remember, Godly men and women encourage, serve, and extend mercy regardless of the situation. These are just a few of God's character traits designed for married couples. How many of us need lasting joy in our lives? All work and no play is never good! God's Word says a merry heart is good for us! Joy when there is no reason to be joyous is definitely prospering! As we are tossed to and fro through this life, it is the Designers' plan to prosper us in many ways! Just as the designer of the washing machine planned it to properly clean our clothes through special cycles (e.g., delicate, heavy, whites) depending on the need of that load, the Designer of marriage has done precisely the same for us. He takes special care in implementing His plans to accommodate each uniquely-designed couple.

No doubt, as we walk through this thing called life, we will end up with some form of harm or discomfort at some point. However, it is not God's original plan! Adam and Eve brought sin into this world, and we feel the results of that sin in our everyday lives. We must remember we have an Elder Brother, Jesus Christ, who provided a way for us to live a life filled with endless possibilities by taking on our sins at the Cross. As married couples, we are to help each other as we walk through our lives. We do not have to face difficulties alone; even the toughest of trials are eased when dealing with them together as one. Instead of allowing the dirt and filth of this world to separate us as couples, we should follow the Designer's plans to attack those challenges together, united as one. Each one of us in our relationships has different strengths and weaknesses. If we will utilize these strengths and weaknesses against the assaults as one, we will be standing at the end of our battles!

"Hope deferred makes the heart sick" (Proverbs 13:12). There is not one person living on this earth that does not need hope. Without hope, we have a tendency to look primarily at the negative issues of our lives. God states clearly that He is giving us a "hope" in Jeremiah 29:11. We cannot have this hope if we do not know the promises of His Word! It is His Word that brings hope into each of our challenges. God's promises fill our hearts with hope. It is when we have this hope that we expect and desire for something good to happen. For example, God states that He will reward those who diligently seek Him. Consequently, as we study His word, pray, worship Him, and seek after Him, we can have the hope that He will reward us just as He says He will. "God is not a man that He should lie" (Numbers 23:19). As couples we share many hopes and dreams; we need to make sure that all of these hopes and dreams line up with God's design for our marriages! Simply put, our hopes and dreams should be in Him and Him alone!

God also promises to give us a "future." It is time in our marriages that we pursue the Designer's future plans for us. God never designed marriage to fail. As Jimmy Evans of Marriage Today has stated numerous times, "We have a 100 percent success rate in marriage if we both will follow God's plans for marriage." Failing marriages were never the intent of God. Quite the contrary, He designed marriage because it was not good for Adam to be alone. When we think about the word "future," we know it is something that has not happened yet. Can we really conclude that God created woman only to remove her from man once they united? No, absolutely not! Adam and Eve were given a future—and a great one—until they sinned!

As married couples, we need to walk in unity as one, knowing with God as our headship, we have bright futures ahead. When we are truly walking with God, we do not need to worry about our futures. Matthew 6:34 states, "Therefore do not worry about tomorrow, for tomorrow will worry about its own things. Sufficient for the day is its own trouble." God holds our pasts, presents, and futures. We can rest assured He has very good futures planned for us.

Please do not confuse what we are saying here to mean our marriages are going to be a tiptoe through the roses with no thorns. Sorry, friends, that is simply not going to happen. What is going to happen is when the dirt and filth of this world come into our marriages and attack our relationships, we pull out our spot cleaner, Resolve, better known to us as the Holy Spirit! We will let the Holy Spirit loose on those spots and watch them disappear. The greatest thing about our Resolve, Holy Spirit, is that the bottle never runs out. We are always equipped for the next stain that tries to attach itself to us!

As we inspect the DESIGN of our marriages, we need to keep in the forefront of our minds that no matter what anyone says, God and God alone designed the institute of marriage. And He designed marriage to be successful and beautiful. As we encounter stresses in our relationships, we will only receive complete cleansing when we consult the original Designer and His plans. Just as when we purchase a new article of clothing, we read the instructions on how to care for this item. God's Word has every instruction needed as to how we are to care for our marriages. His plan is not to harm us; His plan is to prosper us. His plan is to give us a hope and His plan is to give us a future. What great plans and promises!

CHAPTER SEVEN

EXPECT

As we finish up how we can EXPLODE our relationships, let's discuss **EXPECTATIONS.** According to the definition of expectations in *Merriam-Webster's Collegiate Dictionary*, it means "a belief that something will happen or is likely to happen." One distinction we would like to make is between expecting and hoping. Expecting something to happen means a strong possibility, even sometimes with certainty. However, a hope is just a mere possibility without anything promised. Hope is just a strong desire that something will happen. All of us who have been involved in relationships have encountered some form of expectations. We are all raised with expectations from our parents. As we grow up, our parents expect us to mature. In other words, our behaviors, thought processes, and vocabulary at age five should be noticeably different than when we reach thirteen. If not, there is a problem that needs to be addressed. As we become Believers in Christ, God also expects us to mature. We should show growth in our walks with God, becoming more like Christ as the years continue.

Many of us come into marriage with our own expectations about marriage. These can be positive or negative expectations. If we grew up in a very loving and peaceful home with parents who displayed affection for one another, then we most likely expect our marriages to be pleasant experiences. However, if we grew up with parents who were chaotic, angry, and disconnected, we most likely have low or negative expectations of our marriages.

Regardless of whether we have positive or negative views of marriage prior to marrying, those expectations will definitely affect or infect our relationships. If we come into the relationship expecting Ward and June Cleaver to develop and instead get some form of a Jerry Springer couple, we are going to be very disappointed! At the same time, if we are expecting dysfunctional relationships but we marry mates who truly desire to have great relationships and want to work at it, we may be so jaded that we cannot possibly enjoy the relationships. Unfortunately, many of our preconceived expectations set us up for tremendous failures.

Obviously, when we marry we expect our mates to be loving, kind, generous, and faithful. Why do we expect such behaviors? Simple. When we were dating, they were this way. To be honest, whenever any of us places expectations on individuals, we always set ourselves up for potential disappointments.

For example, say someone received a gift, and they thanked the individual for the gift. Suppose the person giving the gift had an expectation of a "proper" thank you and the manner in which they received their thank you was not what they expected. Therefore, the gift-giver left feeling that the gift-receiver was not very appreciative, which simply was not the case. We place so many expectations on others that we honestly do not realize it unless it is brought to our attention. It has become common practice in the world we live in today. It makes sense then that when we inundate our mates with *unrealistic* expectations, and those expectations are not met, we have troubles.

There truly is only one expectation that we can never be disappointed in, and that is God's Word. God's Word is full of promises for us. It spells them out clearly: "If you do this, then I will do this." When God says it, you can take it to the bank. On the other hand, we are simply human beings that cannot please everyone, nor make good on every promise we make. We have a selfish nature and constantly have to push that nature down so the Holy Spirit can take control.

Let's say our mates have spent all day at the office "putting out fires" and trying to please their bosses and their customers. As they walk through the door at home, we are expecting a warm fuzzy greeting. If we do not get one, we have just been let down. Now, was this intentional on your mate's part? Absolutely not! However, many disagreements, heavy debates, arguments, strong conversations, call them what you want, have evolved from this simple scenario. Due to our expectations not being met, our entire evenings have been altered. We are left feeling rejected, and they are left wondering what just happened.

It is unfair of us to judge our spouses because they do not meet our expectations. However, this judging is done routinely in relationships. Not one of us will ever be able to meet our spouses' expectations 100 percent of the time. This is when we go back to the Designer of marriage, God. If we will put ALL of our expectations in His Word, we will not be disappointed. God ALWAYS does what He says He will do. Numbers 23:19 says, "God is not human, that he should lie, not a human being, that he should change his mind. Does he speak and then not act? Does he promise and not fulfill?" (NIV). God is ALWAYS available, as noted in Jeremiah 33:3, "Call to me and I will answer you."

One thing is for sure: this world will NEVER be able to make good on all the promises that are tossed around. Think about the lines we are given on a daily basis: drink this drink for ten days, and lose two dress sizes; take this protein powder with no exercise needed, and you will bulk up. This perfume will keep him attentive to you and only you; follow this five-step plan, and get out of debt in three weeks. Get the picture?

Sad to say, many of us fall for a lot of these marketing concepts, and when our expectations are not met, we get disappointed and angry. Due to the constant barrage of marketing hype, of which many are sexually driven, we have a tendency to carry some of this over into our relationships. Consequently, when our mates are not responding like they are "supposed to," we blame our mates. They are now the problems because our expectations (at least what the marketer implied) has not been met. This problem is very subtle as it creeps into our relationships today, so we all need to examine where our expectations are igniting from. We must pray and ask God to help us release our spouses from our expectations. As we learn God's Word, we will enjoy plenty of things that we can expect to happen, and guess what? They will happen because God and God alone cannot and will not disappoint us!

In our relationships, we must be given the freedom to be the unique and individual couples we have been created to be. We cannot "cookie cutter" our mates, nor should we want to. What a boring world we would live in if we were all the same. Every one of us has been blessed with very unique spouses. We should inspire our spouses to search out what God's design for their lives individually entails and help them achieve His purposes and plans for them. Walking on His pathway will enable them to grow into the best mates any of us could imagine.

Together as couples, we need to pursue what God's purposes and plans are for us. God has given each couple a unique pathway, and when we travel this path together, our relationships exude all the joy and beauty the Designer intended for us. As we wash clothes (yes, another laundry story), we expect our clothing to come out of the washer clean and ready for the dryer. There are those occasions that a few items may not get clean. Our expectations of having clean clothes have not been met by the washing machine. However, we do not start arguing with the machine, kicking it, and replacing it. No, we simply try washing the clothes again. This, our dear friends, is what we do in our marriages. Try, try, and try again. Never, never, never QUIT!

Afterword

As we have laid out in this book, we can have a positive effect on our marriages when we EXPLODE our relationships using the true Designer's plan. It is this positive effect that we are after. We used the word EXPLODE because after an explosion, we are many times rebuilding something bigger and better than the original structure. We are always looking to build stronger foundations, bigger buildings with much more detail and beauty. This is what we want in our marriages today as well.

In order to genuinely achieve changes that are everlasting, we must discard the preconceived notions and worldly influences that have helped so many marriages, quite frankly, fail today. When we truly accept the fact that God is the Designer of marriage, then it is a no brainer . . . doing marriage God's way is the ONLY way to receive its full benefits!

Possibly you are a couple pleased with your relationship and desiring nothing more. If that is you, Praise God. Let your relationship be an encouragement to all those you meet. If, on the other hand, you enjoy your marriage and feel blessed by it but are wanting ALL, EVERYTHING that you are entitled to according to God's design of marriage, then go directly to His Word for your answers and benefits! It is foolish to think that anyone who has a lack of knowledge of God's design for marriage will be able to assist you in journeying through those tough times. They might be able to provide temporary relief, but we are after permanent, rock-solid relationships. We all will walk through challenges, stresses, and difficulties as couples. What makes the difference is **HOW** we choose to walk through those times.

Choosing to journey on the Designer's pathway of marriage will give us the outcome originally intended by the Designer. This is an intentional choice that we as couples must make. Oh, how those of us who are older wish we would have heard and followed God's design from the day of "I do." Matter of fact, it would have been more beneficial to have known the Designer's plans prior to our selections of mates, period! The greatest thing about God's design is that it is never too late to make an about-face right where you are and start following His plan. There is no "update" required to His plan. It remains the same as originally created and still has great success even today!

This book is by no means a complete guide to all of God's designs for our marriages. The intent of this book is to promote us as couples to know with certainty that our marriages are blessings. Marriage is a beautiful relationship between a man and a woman who by God's divine plan become one. Marriage is a union to be cherished and honored. Beautiful marriages can and do exist today.

One closing laundry example: there is no doubt that our laundry will have a much different outcome if we do not sort our clothes, if we select the wrong cycle, or if we select the wrong temperature. Many of us have learned this the hard way. A once nice, white t-shirt is now pink and will only fit our little four-pound Chihuahua. This is exactly what happens to our marriages when we select the wrong source for our guidance. Our relationships are special and unique, so we need to head straight to the Designer, God, and allow Him to lead us into all truth!

It is our hearts' desire to help strengthen relationships no matter what stage they are in: seriously dating, engaged, or newly married. With God, all things are possible, especially strong, exciting, and enjoyable marriages.

We trust that knowledge has been poured into each individual who has read this book. If you would like to be challenged more to achieve all God has for you in your relationship or want more information about Pitcher Ministries Inc., "Pouring God's Design into Relationships," please visit us at www.pitcherministries.org.

Bibliography

Biblica, *New International Version Holy Bible.* Grand Rapids: Zondervan, 2015.

Eggerichs, Emerson, *Love and Respect.* Nashville: W. Publishing Group, 2005.

Evans, Jimmy, and Frank Martin. *The Right One.* Nashville: Thomas Nelson Inc. Publishers, 2015.

Merriam-Webster, *Merriam-Webster's Collegiate Dictionary, 11th Edition.* Springfield: Merriam-Webster, Incorporated, 2008.

Holman Bible Staff, *Holman Christian Standard Bible.* Nashville: Holman Bible Publishers, 2016.

Thomas Nelson, *New King James Version Holy Bible*, Nashville: Thomas Nelson, 1982.

Dear Reader,

We hope that *Not Just Another Marriage Book: Explode Your Relationship* has encouraged you to pursue God's perfect and lasting design for your marriage. Our small book is part of our big efforts at Pitcher Ministries to help reverse the decline of the family unit.

Let us tell you a little about Pitcher Ministries Inc. It was formed through a calling on both of us to serve as an additional instrument for the church in protecting families. At the core of our mission are two beliefs: (1) the forefront of a relationship is key to a successful long-lasting marriage; and (2) a continued "intentional" education and nurturing of the marriage must be top priority for the years ahead. Pitcher Ministries is dedicated to equipping couples to not only form and maintain long-lasting relationships, but to enjoy those relationships as God originally intended.

We are humbled and grateful for the call the Lord has placed on our lives in the formation of Pitcher Ministries Inc. Both of us are all too familiar with the destruction of divorce, having experienced this failure in our own lives.

It is true that we serve a God of great grace—we have received this grace. Divorce is not God's "perfect will" for any couple, a truth that is confirmed by Matthew 19:8: "it was not this way from the beginning." However, God is using our past pain, guilt, and shame from divorce and allowing Romans 8:28 to be displayed in our lives today. As we reach couples through our transparent message of "Pouring God's Design into Relationships," the enemy is defeated.

We look forward to an opportunity to partner with your organization as we explode relationships for eternity. Please contact us at:

Pitcher Ministries
832.945.5323
contact@pitcherministries.org
www.pitcherministries.org
24200 Southwest Fwy, Ste. 402-139
Rosenberg, Texas 77471

Blessings,
Doug and Sissy Pitcher

About the Authors

Doug and Elizabeth (Sissy) Pitcher are delighted to publish their first book focusing on solidifying couples' relationships prior to marriage and during their married years. Doug was born and raised in Eugene, Oregon, while Sissy is a native of Houston, Texas. After both going through the painful process of divorce, they were blessed with finding one another and growing in a very fulfilling marriage. The time is now to step out and fulfill their calling to help build strong and lasting relationships through the education of God's Word.

The Pitchers are *Marriage on the Rock* certified leaders through Jimmy Evans of Marriage Today as well as licensed ministers through The Freedom Center Church in Missouri City, Texas. They are service providers for Twogether in Texas. Doug and Sissy have facilitated Marriage Enrichment workshops, study of *The Right One* (Evans & Martin, 2015), and 2B1 Marriage Ministry meetings as well as pre-marriage preparation for individual couples. They are also certified Single Parent and Stepfamily instructors. The Pitchers' combination of church involvement and leadership roles has equipped them to pursue their calling of Pitcher Ministries Inc. and "Pouring God's Design into Relationships."

Doug and Sissy reside in Rosenberg, Texas, and attend The Freedom Center Church in Missouri City, Texas. They are proud parents to six adult children and are blessed with five beautiful grandchildren.

As they provide an additional instrument for the body of Believers, Pitcher Ministries is available to host meetings in any area and welcomes the opportunity to help strengthen and educate future and established marriages. To contact Doug and Sissy, visit **www.pitcherministries.org**.